Inspired Teaching

Inspired Teaching

✦

A tool kit for new teachers, a reference book for seasoned teachers

Charles Buchheim

iUniverse, Inc.
New York   Bloomington

IT
Inspired Teaching

iUniverse books may be ordered through booksellers or by contacting:

iUniverse
1663 Liberty Drive
Bloomington, IN 47403
www.iuniverse.com
1-800-Authors (1-800-288-4677)

Because of the dynamic nature of the Internet, any Web addresses or links contained in this book may have changed since publication and may no longer be valid.

ISBN: 978-0-595-51384-0 (sc)
ISBN: 978-0-595-61875-0 (ebk)

Printed in the United States of America

iUniverse rev. date: 2/3/2010

My first book is dedicated to my wife, Judy, daughter Jessie, son-in-law Rocco, son Jeff, and daughter-in-law Lisa for believing in me and their continued encouragement.

Special thanks to John Zeck, for his professional feedback and technical assistance in writing and rewriting the "TIPS" articles.

Inspired Teaching is also dedicated to the professionals who have mentored and inspired me over the years, like my mother Olga Buchheim, grandfather Harry Zutch, high school English teacher Ms. Kinsman, department supervisor Mr. Weghorst, and the many hardworking and caring teachers I've had the honor to work alongside for thirty-four years.

A special thank you goes out to my dear friend Victoria Gaunt, for reminding me of the important role substitute teachers play in our schools everyday. So I dedicate chapter 40 to Victoria.

I believe Inspired Teaching is a book every new teacher must have in his or her professional library. Inspired Teaching is also the perfect reference book for the seasoned instructor and administrator.

Contents

Now let *your*

Inspired Teaching

begin!

Preface

My first book is a collection of educational articles I wrote over a ten-year period. With the encouragement of several colleagues, I decided to bring these articles on effective educational strategies to other educators. Once the collection was completed, the most challenging decision was coming up with a title for the book. I wanted a title that would capture the curiosity of readers, in the hope that they would stop, pick up the book, and take the time to read it.

I began to examine my own teaching career, in hopes that a title for my first book would emerge. As I looked back over my career in education, I concluded that I had experienced success in my career because of my ability to adapt instructional strategies to meet the needs of students. These adaptations resulted in large part from my observations of the master teachers around me, as well as numerous professional development sessions. With additional help from a sprinkle of daily enthusiasm and a deep desire to make learning enjoyable, I developed the tools needed to help guide my students toward more effective learning. This reflection revealed my book's title: *Inspired Teaching.*

My career began in a very upper-middle-class community where approximately 75 percent of graduates went on to a community college or four-year college. After two years, I took a position in a middle-class community where half of the graduates entered college and the other half joined the workforce. My final school was a vocational/technical high school where most (80 percent) of my students came from the inner city. This is where I came to truly realize how deep a teacher's teaching strategies needed to be to draw every student into the circle of success. The chapters in this book are a direct reflection of the techniques that have proven to be effective over the years; I wanted to share them with current and future teachers.

Inspired Teaching focuses on providing the new teacher with an array of strategies that, when properly implemented, can enhance the teacher's effectiveness in both the classroom and school communities, which in turn should improve each student's level of success. The seasoned teacher and administrator can rely on this book as a resource for enriching collegiality amongst their peers.

Chapter 1

✦

The Power to Influence Young Minds

○ ○

Nothing can stop the person with the right mental attitude from achieving their goal.

—*Thomas Jefferson*

You've had the summer to relax, unwind, and gather your thoughts for the beginning of the new school year. This chapter focuses on suggestions that can improve the effectiveness of instruction, as well as elevate the success of each student.

Here is one approach to teaching: Start every day by stopping and thinking, *I have the power to influence what happens in my classroom: how the students view themselves, how they view learning, how they view whether what they're doing is meaningful. I'll try to focus on that every day.*

Below are some suggestions to kick off the school year. It is imperative that teachers utilize these ideas throughout the year, not just on opening day. Select strategies that fit your students' learning styles, and don't be afraid to drop strategies that aren't working in favor of new methods.

 Out These Suggestions

Get organized Put all of your materials in order. When instructional materials, notes, equipment, reference books, etc., are in order, the day, week, month, and year go more smoothly.

Introduce yourself Share an autobiographical sketch with your classes. Include your hobbies, activities you like to do outside of school, a little about your family, your life experiences, etc.

Make a good impression Show your students that you are prepared.

Establish rules with your students and then post them.

Be clear Tell your students exactly what you expect of them. (You may wish to hand out written copies of your expectations to be placed into student notebooks.) Provide examples: for instance, be on time to class; complete assignments; have all necessary books and materials with you in class; respect your classmates and instructor, and they will respect you too.

Learn your students' names This demonstrates that you care about each student as an individual.

Cultivate curiosity Present learning puzzles in your activities. Give your students a sampling of the many things they will experience in your class. Encourage them to take risks by praising their daily efforts.

Be focused Always work toward class and individual student goals.

Start slowly This ensures that everyone understands and can experience success.

Buddy up students Identify a classmate who will offer positive daily support as a second resource person. It's imperative that you know the learning styles of each student, along with each personality, so you can effectively pair students during group activities.

Get parents involved Communicate via telephone and/or letters (e-mails are also very effective means of communication) so parents will learn how they can become involved in their child's education. When parents are involved in their child's learning, the student tends to work harder in school.

Stay in touch Establish a communication system with your students and their parents, as well as fellow teachers, guidance staff, and administration. This can be accomplished by talking to parents at school functions (not always about what's taking place in the classroom), sending letters home to the parents, e-mailing messages on a regular basis (good as well as bad news or concerns), a brief telephone call, etc.

Be positive Send positive verbal comments out into the classroom, as well as positive notes home to Mom, Dad, and guardians.

Build spirit Find something unique about each class and promote it. Identify their interests (music, drama, athletics, art, etc.) and incorporate learning activities that enable them to engage these special talents.

Decorate your classroom to catch and keep your students' attention each and every day.

Be prepared for students with special needs (with and without an aide). Adjust your assignments or learning activities. Every class doesn't have to do the same problem or activity to acquire the specific knowledge or skill that week.

Build relationships Get involved in your school's activities. Your students appreciate seeing you at their after-school activities.

Be proud Take pride in your students' accomplishments—and your own. Set aside a bulletin board for student accomplishments that take place outside your classroom, to showcase their other positive sides.

Treat all students equally Fairness and consistency are imperative if you hope to reach your students. They notice and remember how you treat them, as well as the other students in class.

Teach bell to bell Your students deserve a complete education. Don't cut them short by cutting short the lesson or activity. Every minute counts!

Keep a sense of humor!

The heart of schooling is found in relationships between the student, the teacher, and ideas. Every student differs, and ideas affect each one in a different way. You can't teach a student well if you don't know your student well. As you get a handle on each student's learning style, adapt your learning activities accordingly.

Chapter 2

♦

Powerful Instruction

o o o o o o o o o o o o o o o o o o o o o o o o o o o o o o
It's hard for an empty sack to stand upright.

—Ben Franklin

Dr. Margaret C. Wang, past director of the Laboratory for Student Success at Temple University, introduced the phrase Powerful Instruction. *She defines powerful instruction as the daily improvement of the students' knowledge base. Simply put, if a student walks out of a classroom without increasing his or her knowledge from the previous day, powerful instruction is not happening.*

Four factors have a direct impact on the quality of instruction in a school. Let's examine these factors that promote powerful instruction.

Classroom control is the number one factor that impacts the quality of instruction. The effective teacher has mastered the art of good classroom management. She establishes a classroom environment conducive to learning, a place where everyone is encouraged to share ideas or opinions in a way that isn't offensive.

The master teacher **incorporates an assortment of teaching strategies**. Don't do the same thing day-in and day-out. If you take that tired approach, you can count on little learning taking place and constant classroom disruption.

Utilize varied student-centered learning activities. This strategy increases the chances of improving student motivation in the classroom.

Carefully examine your instructional techniques and the types of student activities you use throughout the period, week, month, and year. Are you incorporating varied and effective teaching strategies, as well as numerous types of student-centered learning activities? The answer needs to be yes, if you expect your students to be engaged in real learning every day.

One other factor greatly affects the level of learning: ***teacher-with-it-ness***, or understanding the student's individual learning styles and interests. If you fail to design learning activities that hook each student, you're wasting your time and your student's time. It takes a lot of effort on your part to design high-caliber lessons, but in the long run that's what we should expect from ourselves as professionals. Your students will appreciate it as well, and genuine powerful instruction will take place. Challenge yourself to really get to know each student you teach. Design teaching strategies and learning activities that help every student make the connection to the learning taking place.

Our students need to know that we regard what occurs in the classroom very seriously and that we're ready to help them find success. By making six simple statements to your students, you can help them ensure a great school year.

Share these six important statements with your students, and encourage open and frank discussion about these points.

1. I want to be here.
2. I want you to be here.
3. I'm excited about getting started.
4. I'm enthusiastic and optimistic about the learning opportunities we'll have.
5. You are important.
6. I am here to help you succeed … all of you.

Starting the school year off with these six statements can provide the foundation needed for delivering more powerful instruction. I encourage you to embrace the idea that powerful instruction is the number one goal.

Chapter 3

✦

Now That's Assessment: Vary Your Strategies

○ ○
Encouragement is the oxygen to the soul.
—George M. Adams

When teachers expand and reformulate our views of what counts as human intellect, we become able to design more effective ways of assessing learners and more appropriate ways of educating them. One way to improve our students' level of success is by designing our lessons with the end in mind. Your first reaction to that statement might be, "That doesn't make sense." In reality, it makes all the sense in the world; how can we determine what our students need to know or be able to do if we don't know what the end result needs to be?

So, it becomes quite evident that as teachers, we need to look at where we want our students to be at the end of the school year, based on several factors, including state standards, the district curriculum, and where our students' levels of understanding or knowledge base exist in relation to the discipline we are teaching. By reflecting on these key factors, we can identify the essential or critical learning to be addressed. Design and utilize an assessment tool to be used at the start of the school year to determine exactly where your students' levels of understanding or knowledge are to find the true starting point.

Once you've determined what the outcome by the end of the school year needs to be and identified the essential lessons and learning activities, the final piece of the puzzle needs to be put into place. That final and very important component is assessment. Sometimes we get into the routine of determining a student's level of understanding based on soft data (verbal response, show of hands, attentiveness in class, just to name a few). However, the best way to assess a student's true level of understanding is to incorporate multiple forms of assessment in the classroom. A varied assessment method requires the teacher to combine multiple daily methods of assessment: **observation** of processes by the teacher (student presentations, students reading aloud, student questions, hands-on activities, discussion, debate, etc.); **conversation** between teacher and student to pull responses that will clearly indicate the student's level of understanding; and **collection of products** (draw a diagram, draw a picture, make a poster, write a report, test/quiz, make a video, create a collage, a journal entry, project, etc.).

It takes some planning to make sure you have enough evidence, the right kind of evidence (data that clearly identifies what the student knows and understands. For example, if the outcome is for a student to prove he or she knows the difference between a parallel and series circuit, the student must correctly build both circuits and demonstrate how they work to the instructor), and reliable and valid evidence (meaning the assessment tools are a true reflection of the critical learning that needs to be understood).

How much evidence is enough?

There is no one right answer to this question. The amount of ongoing evidence needed to effectively plan day-to-day instruction will vary from teacher to teacher, and subject to subject. The best way to determine how often and how much evidence is enough is to keep in mind at all times the desired end result, and to always incorporate a varied assessment process.

How do I know I have the right kinds of evidence?

The types of assessments you use need to be appropriate to the type of learning taking place in the subject area. For example, a paper test is a great way to assess knowledge of basic facts. It wouldn't be an appropriate way to assess a student's oral communications, or to demonstrate that the student knows the proper steps to complete a science lab or to produce a series versus parallel circuit in electrical class. Select various forms of assessment that will provide you with genuine evidence of learning or understanding. Assessment needs to take place in the classroom day in and day out, and it must vary so as not to bore the students or become routine.

When teachers collect enough of the right kind of evidence, then we can feel confident evaluations will be reliable and valid. The right kind of evidence is that which clearly shows the student has indeed mastered the required skill or knowledge in a way that he or she can correctly replicate the task.

Chapter 4

✦

Connecting Learning to Students

o o o o o o o o o o o o o o o o o o o o o o o o o o o o o o

If a child lives with praise, she learns to appreciate.
                                                    —*Dorothy Nolte*

Learning is a process of making meaning out of new or unfamiliar events or activities in conjunction with familiar ideas, understandings, or experiences. Learners construct knowledge as they build cognitive maps to organize and interpret new information. Effective teachers help students develop these maps by making connections among different concepts and between new ideas and the learner's prior experiences.

Children learn best when new ideas are presented in a way that provides the learner with ways that connect to his/her motivation and prior knowledge; teachers need to respond to the challenges and questions their students raise. As educators we must become experts at observing how each student thinks and reacts to dialogue, tasks, and interactions with their classmates and instructor. Some students need visuals to make the connection, while others need to repeat the learning task several times before the light clicks on for that student. Others may require one-on-one dialogue with the instructor so their individual questions can be examined and clarified. We must be able to adjust the learning activities at a moments notice to insure every student is connected.

One key to student development is providing clear standards and criteria for performance on specific tasks, linked to lots of feedback. Make sure you continually get feedback from your students. One way is to incorporate the ten-two technique in your daily classroom assessment activities (for every ten minutes of learning activities, the instructor needs to provide students at least two minutes of feedback to assess their level of understanding). Students also need access to examples of high-quality work that they can use as models. Additionally, we must constantly incorporate active learning into every lesson. As the old saying goes, "I hear and I forget; I see and I remember; I do and I understand."

So, if our goal is getting our students connected to learning, real learning, we must engage students in critical thinking and production. Tasks should represent real-life situations when possible to keep student motivation high. Have students design, conduct, and analyze an experiment; interpret a piece of literature; or develop a hypothesis, rather than complete a canned lab experiment. Work that results in deep understanding has the greatest chance of becoming embedded in that student's mind forever.

Chapter 5

♦

Getting Parents Involved in the School Community

○ ○

A parent is a child's first teacher.

—Jacquie McTaggart

If we look back over the years and begin to think about our most successful students, it becomes clear that many factors contributed to his or her success in school. One necessary ingredient is parental involvement. Unfortunately, the level of parental involvement seems to diminish when children enter their high school years.

Here are some strategies teachers and schools can use to improve parental participation:

- Develop and publicize a plan to promote parent and community involvement. Post calendars of committee meetings and school activities for the year, as well as the school e-mail addresses for every teacher, counselor, and administrator.
- Foster a climate of hospitality and openness that gives parents and others the information and confidence they need to become actively involved in school activities.
- Focus on the needs of parents and community members, not on the needs of the school and its personnel alone.
- Build a personal knowledge base of parental and community member occupations, interests, and affiliations to assist with the school's inclusion of parents and community.

- Target specific parents and community members for tasks and issues in which they have both the interest and the experience to be a positive and effective contributor. Recruit parents and people in the business community to play a role in developing curriculum, identifying technology upgrades, and procuring donations from the community and/or business community.
- Use your encounters with parents and community members as opportunities to develop positive two-way communications.
- Have conversations with the students in your classes in an effort to identify parents willing to participate on school committees. Ask students to take a form home for their parents to complete concerning participation on key committees in the district, based on parent interest and professional experience.
- Respect the cultural sensitivities and life experiences of your students, their parents, and family.
- Make an effort whenever possible to reach out and communicate with parents for reasons other than feedback sessions about their child's performance in your classroom. Invite parents as guest speakers, to accompany students on class trips, to be a member of a panel in your classroom, etc.
- Link some of your classroom learning activities with experiences that draw on family and/or community interests.
- Send positive communications home to parents about their child via a handwritten note or e-mail.
- Enter parent conferences with a willingness to carefully listen to the parents concerns, as well as effectively express your expectations. The goal is to finish with a win-win outcome.

Our job as educators can be a little bit easier if we have the involvement and support of our students' parents. We need to accept the fact that our job doesn't end at the classroom door, but should extend beyond that doorway. When parents feel that their input is valued, they will play a more active role in their child's education.

Chapter 6

✦

Commitment Breeds Success

○ ○
Look to the experiences of others to guide and inspire you.
—*Unknown*

What is commitment? This word has different meanings for different people:

- To the boxer, it's getting off the mat once more than your opponent.

- To the soldier, it's going over the hill, not knowing what's waiting on the other side.

- To the teacher, it's not giving up on your students, even when it seems like the students have given up on themselves.

True commitment inspires you as well as the people around you. President John F. Kennedy believed the United States of America could place a man on the moon and return him safely to Earth. His commitment to this dream motivated others, and thus his dream became a reality. Thomas Edison believed he could produce light using electricity, which inspired the invention of the light bulb. Although numerous attempts to make the light bulb failed, his commitment finally made the electric light bulb a reality. So, what is the true nature of commitment? Three levels of commitment must be practiced if teachers wish to attain their goals in the classroom.

- Commitment starts in the **heart**. If you want to achieve your goals and the goals of the school district, the commitment begins inside each and every one of us. We must be advocates for genuine student learning. If that commitment is not embedded in our hearts, we're in the wrong profession and need to step aside for others to lead the way.

- Commitment is tested by our **actions**. It's one thing to talk about commitment. It's another to do something about it. The only real measure of commitment is action. Arthur Gordon once said, "Nothing is easier than saying words. Nothing is harder than living them day after day."

- Commitment breeds **achievement**. You will face many obstacles and much opposition along the way, and there will be times when commitment is the only thing that carries you forward. Remember that commitment is the enemy of resistance, for it is the serious promise to press on, to get back up, no matter how many times you are knocked down.

If we want to achieve our goals we must be committed. As Winston Churchill once said, "Never give up, never give up!"

To improve your commitment, do the following:

- List your goals You need to identify your goals so you know what your daily objectives must be to achieve that goal. The first step is to understand the end result that you and the district are trying to achieve.
- Make your plans public. Place your plans and goals for the school year on the bulletin board for all to see. List the skills and knowledge your students will be expected to acquire by the end of the school year. Break down benchmarks by months and weeks that you and your students need to attain in order to reach the end-of-year goal. By making your plans public, you will be more committed to follow through with them, and so will your students.
- Measure your true level of commitment. Take a few minutes at the end of your workday and tally up how many ways you believe you succeeded at enriching the lives of your students and colleagues.

Be committed, and success will be your friend.

Chapter 7

✦

Conflict Resolution

This chapter title sounds like an oxymoron, doesn't it? We observe conflict in our classrooms, hallways, homes, and communities each and every day. As educators, we are called upon daily to implement corrective action that will resolve conflict(s).

Over time, teachers have come to understand that dealing with conflict in a constructive manner not only benefits our sense of harmony and compatibility, but it also challenges us to find inventive answers to our differences through effective communication.

Here are some proactive steps that you can use to successfully resolve conflict:

- Stay calm and rational. This not only allows you to think more clearly but also increases the chances the other person or persons will act in a similar manner. Use direct eye contact and speak clearly, but do not yell or use inappropriate language. Always maintain a professional demeanor.
- Adopt a positive frame of mind. Focus on gains instead of losses. Students (especially teens) hear way too much negative language directed at them. They could use positive stimulation through your verbal encouragement in the classroom.
- Remember that the person on the other side of a conflict has a point of view that is just as legitimate and reasonable to him or her as

yours is to you. Provide a place (whether in the classroom, hallway, or office) where all sides can be heard before determining the best resolution to the conflict.

- Indicate that you understand the other person's perspective. This validates their argumentativeness and allows them to believe in your objectivity and sincerity. When students vent, it is important that you look directly at them and not interrupt. It's not easy but is vital to the process.

- Acknowledge that the other person may also be uncomfortable about the conflict and want to see it resolved. Young people don't want or like conflict either. Many times the cause of the conflict has to do with personal relations between the two students in conflict. Identify the cause, and you're on the road to resolving the problem.

- Be willing to make concessions (when able). Focus on win-win conclusions for all parties. When students can look at each other, smile, and say, "It's over," can you be assured the conflict is truly over?

- Avoid making accusatory statements and negative remarks about any of the students involved in the conflict. Such statements only put people on the defensive and can cause the situation to escalate.

- It is imperative to keep to the issue(s) and avoid arguments that are personal. The tendency (by the students) is to bring up old wounds to justify the current behavior.

- Start with what actually took place and the role each student played in the conflict, and then work together to find a way to resolve the problem and prevent it from occurring in the future.

- Identify a shared goal that will tie the students' interests together. In this way, both parties can benefit. No one walks away from the conflict as the victim or loser.

- The future is a more constructive base for discussion than the past. Therefore, rather than dwelling on what or who caused the conflict, emphasize what can be done to provide a resolution now and into the future.

- Don't major in minors (sometimes we spend way too much time focused on minor details); keep the end in mind always.

Conflict is a part of our daily lives. Utilizing these steps can help us reduce the number of conflicts as well as provide us with a more effective means of preventing conflict in the future.

Chapter 8

◆

Mistakes are Wonderful Learning Experiences

o o o o o o o o o o o o o o o o o o o o o o o o o o o o o

If you give up, you give up on your students. They deserve your perseverance.

—*Charles D. Buchheim*

One of my favorite thoughts comes from Elbert Hubbard, and it goes something like this: "The greatest mistake a person can make is to be afraid of making one." This thought touches me because educators need to realize that students need to make mistakes; these mistakes are sometimes the best learning opportunities they may experience.

When we were learning to walk, how many times did we fail before we were able to take our first successful journey across the kitchen floor? When we received our first bicycle, how many times did we fall before succeeding?

Isn't it true that we learn best through our mistakes? Skinned knees are a necessary part of learning to ride a bike. Burnt meals are a necessary part of learning how to cook. Now think back to your first year of teaching. Did you make mistakes? In fact, no matter how long you've been in education, you'll still make mistakes? Yet our ability to recognize that students will fail before they succeed is sometimes forgotten.

Even though, as adults and educators, we recognize that mistakes are wonderful learning opportunities, this is not always the prevailing message in the classroom. Since making mistakes is one of the ways that we learn, we should encourage our students to take chances, because everyone will learn from it. No student should ever be singled out and embarrassed for making a mistake. The greatest mistake any student can make is to stop trying for fear of failing. That usually occurs when a teacher makes fun of a student for giving a wrong answer. If we want our students to take risks, we have to take the good responses with the bad ones.

An environment conducive to learning is one where students feel comfortable enough to simply do their best, no matter the outcome. In the long run your students will realize that mistakes can be positive learning experiences. Administrators should also want and expect to see students making mistakes, because they too need to adopt the view that students' "getting it wrong" is a wonderful opportunity to enhance individual learning.

Eventually, with guided practice and encouragement, students will be successful. Both the teaching staff and administrative team need to embrace genuine effort from their students, because in the long run students will learn—really learn.

It's important that educators realize the fire we light in our students for learning will affect them for a lifetime. Encourage your students to take a chance, even if they are wrong. Thomas Edison failed over a thousand times before he succeeded in making the light bulb work.

Chapter 9

♦

Motivating Students by Focusing on Their Individuality

○ ○

Never, never, never, never give up.

—Winston Churchill

When it comes to addressing student motivation, *101 Answers for New Teachers and Their Mentors* is a must-read book for educators. Author Annette Breaux is an educator and mentor for teachers in a Louisiana school district. Ms. Breaux's book clarifies how important student motivation is in the classroom.

We all realize that our classes are made up of many students, each with his or her own unique personality and learning style. The art of motivation is a critical skill that teachers must master. I would like to share her view on motivation, which begins with a poem by Ms. Breaux.

I'M NOT MY OLDER BROTHER

I'm not my older brother
So please do not compare
To treat me as another would surely be unfair
He has ways of doing things
Ways that are his own
He's okay, but there's no way
That I'll become his clone
I'm not my older brother

18

and I do not wish to be
I'm happy to be who I am
And that is simply me.

Ms. Breaux points out that as educators, we need to celebrate the uniqueness of our students. Every student is his own person, a unique individual with unique talents, skills, strengths, and dreams. Yet we often try to make our students someone they are not. We compare them to their brother or sister or to other students.

Ask any parent who has two or more children if their children are even remotely alike. The answer will be a resounding "No." Our job, as teachers, is to find the unique aspects of every student we teach and to celebrate those qualities. I am not, of course, referring to a student's unique quality of being the most disruptive person in the classroom. Rather, we need to find his or her strengths and talents and nurture those.

Take those students with a talent for speaking and encourage them to present their reports orally. Allow your artistic students to take turns decorating the bulletin boards in the classroom. It's important to remember that each student is a unique individual, their own person. Treat them that way. Celebrate who they are rather than pushing them to be someone she is not.

Chapter 10

✦

Academic Success Begins with Relationships

People need joy as much as clothing.

—*Margaret Collier Graham*

Establishing positive relationships with students is one way to create a safe and productive learning environment that promotes equality and encourages all students to succeed. To establish such an environment in schools, teachers and administrators must have a broad repertoire of strategies to connect with the diversity of students in their school. What works with one student or one class may not work with others. In addition, what works for some teachers or administrators may not work for others. Building personal relationships is exactly that—personal. How we build those relationships with our students and colleagues will vary with each individual. Build we must!

In the beginning of the school year, and then throughout the course of the year, as the instructor, you must lay the foundation for positive relationships with your students and colleagues. When it comes to your colleagues, get to know them. Especially in your department or grade level, as a starting point and let them know you're eager to share ideas and teaching strategies throughout the school year. When you witness a colleague doing something special or offering an act of kindness, acknowledge it.

The best way to set the foundation in place with your students is to learn their names quickly, and also something about each of them (like the music they listen to; their hobbies; extracurricular activities, they're involved in their community, etc.) Implement a brief list of classroom rules (that your students help develop) that both you and your students must follow.

The administration can and must support the instructor's efforts by providing professional development that reflects the goals of the district for improving instructional strategies geared at improving student learning. Annette Breaux offers practical and doable techniques to implement in the classroom that will enhance your strategies for cultivating effective relationships. Her seminars and workshops focus on practicality and the infusion of personality into our teaching and modeling strategies. Take the initiative and procure a copy of Annette's book *101 Answers for New Teachers and Their Mentors.*

Annette's book offers proven learning strategies that are subject-specific and that encourage the expansion of colleague-to-colleague interaction throughout the school year. Establish cohorts for each discipline so educators have a venue to challenge and push themselves. This will test their metal in tasks that require additional concentration and planning, proactive decision-making, self-reflection, and skillful execution.

As educators, we get to see our students grow physically, mentally, and emotionally during their four years at our schools. They literally change before our eyes. They spend a great deal of time, day-in and day-out, in the school community. If we can successfully establish positive relationships with our students, they will succeed in every endeavor, at our schools and for the rest of their lives. We must be the leaders during these school years. We are the future for our students.

Chapter 11

♦

Worthwhile and Effective Learning Tasks Are Essential

o o o o o o o o o o o o o o o o o o o o o o o o o o o o o o

Much effort, much prosperity.

—*Ben Franklin*

Teachers are responsible for developing quality learning tasks that are close to real-life and interesting for students as possible. A wide range of materials exists for designing and implementing effective learning activities or tasks: textbooks, reference books, computer software, practice sheets, puzzles, and manipulative materials. Include sharing ideas among colleagues within the district and beyond. Some tasks grow out of students' conjectures or questions. Teachers need to choose and develop tasks that are likely to promote the development of students' understandings of concepts, procedures, and/or skills in a way that also fosters their ability to reason, to solve problems, and to communicate at a level that will cause this learning to remain with the student for life.

These kinds of tasks require deep reflection and careful teacher planning. Such lessons also will encourage students to work harder than they've had to in the past. The eventual outcome will be a higher level of understanding that will carry over into future courses and their adult lives. In selecting, adapting, or generating learning tasks, teachers must base their decisions on the subject content and/or standards (refer to the key skills or concepts that your students need to master by the conclusion of the course or school year), the make-up of the students (as instructors we need to have a clear grasp of the intellectual level of the students so we can determine how best to plan and implement learning activities and assessment tools), and the ways in which the students learn (through observation, questions and answers, conversations, and the collection of student work). The tasks need to challenge students to expand their repertoire of thinking skills from the simple understanding or knowledge level up to application, evaluation, analysis, and synthesis. If we want the outcome to be genuine learning, not memorized responses to pass a test, teachers need to design learning tasks that require students to speculate, organize, classify, hypothesize, forecast, compose, conclude, and demonstrate.

Finally, it is imperative that teachers obtain formative feedback from every student every day (by using observation, verbal interaction, Q & A, written work, etc.) as a means of correctly planning what will be taught the next day. This requires teachers to keep in mind what the intended target or end result is and to design questions that support the desired outcome. By initiating and orchestrating effective instructional strategies, learning tasks focused on the final outcome, and meaningful formative and summative assessments (for instance, a formative technique would be to have your student explain the reason for using specific punctuation in a sentence, while a summative technique would be to have your student orally describe all of the factors that caused a specific outcome in a science experiment), students will succeed not only in school, but more importantly, in life.

Chapter 12

✦

Effective Classroom Management: The Key to Powerful Instruction

○ ○
What comes from the heart goes to the heart.
—Samuel Taylor Coleridge

As educators we focus much time and energy on designing and implementing strategies that will create an optimum learning environment. We develop independent guided projects and cooperative learning assignments. We incorporate technology, and even occasionally have students become the teachers.

The one component of a teacher's professional repertoire that may be neglected or given little thought is his or her classroom management strategies. This is unfortunate, because the real key to developing an effective classroom environment is mastering effective classroom management skills. This is achieved when our students feel we truly care about them as much as, if not more, than the subject matter we teach. Until this connection is made, a positive learning environment has little chance for success.

The Center for Research in Human Development and Education conducts an annual national survey of teachers, asking them to identify in priority order the top twenty factors that influence student learning. Every year teachers have selected **classroom management** as number one. This data is collected on a yearly basis by the Center for Advanced Learning on the Temple University campus, located in Philadelphia, Pennsylvania.

Because classroom management is so important, let's take a look at some key steps teachers need to consider.

- Greet your students as they enter your classroom everyday.
- Understand clearly what your students' strengths and weaknesses are and use teaching strategies that build on your students' strengths.
- Know your purpose: student achievement.
- Know how to best utilize your time in the classroom. Be flexible; things will happen in the school day that will force you to adjust on a moment's notice.
- Have a short but clear list of classroom rules that everyone is expected to follow, including the teacher. We are the role models for our students, and our actions speak louder than our words.
- We have an obligation to practice learning strategies that ensure learning success for every child. The philosophy of every teacher must be that every child can and will learn.
- Foster independent learning in the classroom.
- Be prepared for class. Ten seconds of idle time can develop into ten minutes of problems.
- Make your assignments challenging but reasonable—and, most of all, clear.
- Don't punish the entire class for the actions of one or two.
- Never, humiliate a student in front of the entire class.
- Use the telephone to share positive information with parents.
- Be enthusiastic; it's contagious.
- Don't make study a punishment. You cannot motivate a student to "learn a punishment." Think about that statement.

We have all heard ourselves say that students of today are a great challenge. Isn't that why we entered this profession—to take on that very challenge? As educators we have the opportunity to transform that raw talent and energy into the success stories of tomorrow.

Master your classroom management skills, and you will see your students reach their individual and collective dreams.

Chapter 13

✦

Teaching is a Noble Profession

o o o o o o o o o o o o o o o o o o o o o o o o o o o o o
Our task is not to fix blame for the past, but to fix the
course for the future. –

John F. Kennedy

There is a public misconception floating out there that teachers have it
made. Some think that people who could not cut it in the business world
opted to take the easy route and become teachers. Based on my thirty-four
years of experience in the field, nothing could be further from the truth. Don't
get me wrong; I've seen and worked with my share of ineffective teachers, but
they are in the minority. I believe this misperception is caused by the small
failures that the media focuses on, rather than the larger successes that are
occurring every day in our schools. The truth is that teaching is quite possibly
the most demanding of all professions one could pursue. The good news is
that teaching is, without a doubt, the most rewarding and noble profession
of all. We give of ourselves in order to pass onto the next generation the
knowledge and skills necessary to survive in today's world, as well as the
future.

This profession is hard work. Our journey will be rocky at times. We
will stumble and fall on occasion. We may even bleed a little, but we need
to realize that this profession is very worthwhile. The rewards of teaching far
outweigh the demands we must endure each and every day of our career.

Teachers realize this when they get their first bear hug from one of their
students, or as they wipe a tear from a student's cheek with the sleeve of their
shirt, or the first time a student leaves an apple on our desk or a birthday

26

card with a note at the bottom—anytime we witness the slightest or greatest achievements and the least or most concerted efforts from our students.

The greatest challenge we face day-in and day-out is when a student attempts to push our panic button. Professionals will never let themselves get to the point that they lose their professional composure.

As professionals, we need to remind our students that we are their teacher, not their friend. Failing to make and keep that level of understanding can and will create problems. We want our students to feel comfortable around us, but at the same time respect us.

Professional educators have an awesome responsibility to prepare young people to be ready and able to handle the challenges and opportunities they will face the rest of their lives. As professionals, we are expected to get the job done, and so many of us do.

So walk tall, my fellow colleagues, and give your best, day in and day out, because our students deserve it. It's a noble profession because of people like you.

Chapter 14

♦

How Can We Increase Student Motivation?

o o o o o o o o o o o o o o o o o o o o o o o o o o o o o
One of the best ways to persuade others is with your ears.
—*Dean Rusk*

Motivation, a student's drive to learn, is one of the most important factors in successful accomplishments at school, at home, and on the job. It's important we realize that motivation is not generic; it is learned; what is learned can be taught; and teaching is our business. Therefore, teachers need to become knowledgeable about, and skilled in the use of, professional techniques, which have high potential for increasing a student's motivation or intent to learn.

The present is what matters; thus, we need to become aware of three factors that we can modify daily in our classroom. Factors that have the power to increase a student's effort and drive to learn: a student's level of concern: the tone in your classroom: and ensuring that success is a part of every student's day.

Let's examine each of these factors in more depth:

- The first factor you can affect in the classroom is the student's *level of concern* about achieving. In the past, we believed that stress, or concern, was undesirable. Now we know that a moderate level of concern is essential to an individual's effort level. It has been scientifically proven that a moderate level of concern stimulates efforts to learn. When there is no concern, there is little or no learning. When there is too much concern, there may be no energy available for learning.

Some simple but effective techniques used by the instructors already affect the level of motivation to learn in the classroom. As a review, here is a list of some of the tried and true motivational techniques:

> ➢ Standing next to a student who is not participating in a classroom activity can re-focus that student's effort by raising his or her level of concern
> ➢ Announcing to the class, "This will probably be on the next test or quiz"
> ➢ Returning a graded test or project quickly (next day) and reviewing to identify and remedy learning gaps
> ➢ Announcing to the class, "This part of the activity is difficult, so a higher level of concentration and effort is required"
> ➢ Raising the students' level of concern by assigning projects, midterms, or final exams
> ➢ Informing a student that you will be calling home later today to speak with his or her parent

- The *feeling tone* in the classroom or learning environment is the second factor that can have an affect on a student's motivation. The way a student feels in a particular situation affects the amount of effort he or she is willing to put forth to achieve learning. Whether or not you want to acknowledge it, feeling tones exist in every classroom. Obviously, students are most inclined to put forth effort to learn if they find the learning environment pleasant.

- A third and final factor that increases student motivation is the *feeling of success*. In order to feel successful, one must expend effort and achieve a certain degree of accomplishment. The mastery of a new or more difficult skill will always boost the student's feeling of success, in turn increasing his or her level of motivation. Compliment students for their efforts, even if they give the wrong response. Praise the entire class when students are successful in the completion of a difficult assignment.

Teachers need to effectively utilize techniques that incorporate moderate concern, create a positive feeling tone, and establish a place where all students attain success. All three components are needed since they interact with each other, as we need to use them in concert. The master teacher finds a way to build the kind of classroom atmosphere that cultivates student motivation to learn.

Chapter 15

✦

Collaboration Promotes Professional Growth

○ ○

Give to every other human being every right that you claim
for yourself.

—*Robert G. Ingersoll*

Teachers need to become collaborators; they can be allies and mentors
for each other. They can help each other through reflection and dialogue and
the sharing of ideas, techniques, and forms of assessment, to name a few. I
don't believe that people who have not worked in education can comprehend
the intensity of the work, the level of emotional involvement we have with
our students, parents, and colleagues, or the nonstop pace. We need time to
share and decompress in order to be effective day in and day out. Forming
collaborative groups amongst our colleagues is helpful and necessary. There
are times when we feel vulnerable. Forming professional and personal
bonds with our colleagues establishes a network that supports, guides, and
enhances our ability to function in a productive way. A perfect way to form
these groups is to have a team of master teachers mentor teachers new to the
district by providing common prep times. At every faculty meeting, have a
few teachers present a Sharing Session with the staff on unique assessment
techniques, classroom management techniques that are proven winners, and
allow tenured as well as new teachers the opportunity to sit in and observe
colleagues in action in their classrooms.

Because of the physical confines of our classrooms or offices, it is very
easy for teachers or administrators to become isolated from their peers. If we

allow ourselves to become an island in the sea, sooner or later the challenges we must face will seem impossible to handle. By forming collaborative groups, we create a team of experts that brings to the table many experiences and skills necessary to confront challenges head-on and succeed.

The difference between the teacher as a solitary figure behind a closed door and the teacher as steward of a school community involves a profound shift in one's personality and point of view. Administration must support and encourage staff to reach beyond the classroom setting and connect with the resources, experiences, and ideas of fellow colleagues. Become a collaborator, and you will grow in leaps and bounds, professionally and personally!

Chapter 16

◆

Make Every Student Your Favorite

o o o o o o o o o o o o o o o o o o o o o o o o o o o o

Reach out and get to know your students.
—*Charles D. Buchheim*

Make every student your "favorite," is what Annette L. Breaux advises in her book *101 Answers for New Teachers and Their Mentors.* Annette often tells teachers, "If I should walk into ... classrooms and ask who the teacher's favorite student is, all hands should go up. If a few hands remain down, I can practically guarantee that those are the students who tend to cause problems." She goes on to say, "Students who do not feel that you care are the ones most likely to seek your attention in inappropriate ways, as often as possible. The good news is that the opposite is also true. Once a student is convinced that you care about him or her, they will do almost anything to please you."

She will act politely, she will do her work, she will behave appropriately, and she will even turn in homework! It's quite simple; students want to feel successful, appreciated, and respected. Although the task is no small one, you should make it a priority to somehow make each student feel that she is your "secret favorite."

This can be accomplished by taking a personal interest in every student, by making sure that every student is experiencing success, and by doing all the little things that tell students we care about them. Show me a teacher who treats all students as favorites, and I'll show you a classroom with minimal behavior problems and high levels of student achievement. This skill develops from careful observation and keen listening skills on the teacher's part. You may want to designate a section in your plan book (or a separate notebook)

33

for listing a few key interests or special abilities each student has developed or acquired. Use this information to motivate specific students on occasion or to divert one of your students from acting out in a negative way.

Annette reminds all of us how important it is to convey to our students that we are here for them. Help your students to believe that they can, and they will. A student with a positive attitude can and will achieve. As educators, we have the responsibility of bringing out the best in all of our students!

Try making every student your favorite, and see what happens.

Chapter 17

✦

Encourage Improvement, Not Perfection

○ ○

"Nothing has a better effect upon children than praise."
—*Sir P. Sidney*

Did you know that in his career Babe Ruth hit 714 homeruns? He also struck out 1,330 times! In the sport of baseball, many of the great players have made it into the Hall of Fame with a lifetime batting average of three hundred or less. That means that they failed 70 percent of the time. Yet they are considered extremely successful, the best of the best.

In school, however, a student has to succeed at least 70 percent of the time in order to get by with a barely passing grade. Try to imagine any area of your life where you are successful more than 70 percent of the time. I'll bet you'll have a difficult time doing that.

In football, every single play is technically designed to score points. However, almost every play scores no points. That doesn't stop the coach from building on each play that does not score points and trying to turn the next play into a more successful one.

Find a parent who succeeds 70 percent of the time with everything he or she tries to teach their child. That parent does not exist. Better yet, find a stockbroker who succeeds with 70 percent of all his stock investments. If you do, start investing!

The point is that we often label students as failures because we make the mistake of encouraging perfection in all they do. Admit it: if you took a test with a hundred questions and received a grade of 95 percent, you would immediately look for the five that you missed as opposed to the ninety-five that you got right.

In the classroom, we should teach students that improvement is what matters. Most of the time, perfection is nearly impossible. If we focus on striving for continual perfection, it will give us ulcers and drive our students into despair. A healthier approach to learning is seeking steady improvement. As time moves forward, perfection will be reached. Homeruns are great, but strikeouts are more common, and strikeouts provide opportunities for us to improve. An enthusiastic swing and miss has led many people to greatness. Encourage your students to do their best. When you see that they are giving their best effort, provide them encouragement and time to reflect, redo, and try again.

Chapter 18

✦

An Important Lesson in Life

o o o o o o o o o o o o o o o o o o o o o o o o o o o o

If it is to be it is up to me.

—Unknown

Back in 1999, an article appeared in the *Dear Abby* section of a local newspaper that effectively addressed the topic of self-esteem. I was so touched by the story that I cut the article out and saved it to use one day to motivate students I was teaching or staff I was coaching.

Retired Teacher from St. Paul, Minnesota

Dear Abby: I have been retired from teaching for many years and would like to share a lesson I learned that stands out in my memory like no other.

I was young and teaching math at the junior high school level. We had worked hard on a new concept all week and the students were very stressed. They were frowning, frustrated and carping.

Wanting to stop the crankiness before it got out of hand, I asked the students to take out two sheets of paper and list the names of the other students in class, leaving a space between each name. I told them to think of the nicest thing they could say about each of their classmates and write it down. When the students handed me the papers, they seemed more relaxed.

That weekend, I wrote the name of each student on a sheet of paper and listed what the students had said about that individual. On Monday, I gave each student his or her list. Before long, everyone was smiling. "REALLY!" I heard one whisper; "I never knew that meant anything to anyone. I didn't know anyone liked me that much."

The assignment was never mentioned again, but it didn't matter. The exercise had accomplished its purpose. The students felt better about themselves.

Years later, I was asked to attend the funeral of one of those students. I was deeply saddened by his untimely death in Vietnam.

The church was packed with Mark's friends, many of who had been his classmates and students of mine. After the funeral, I and many of Mark's former classmates were invited to his parent's house. Mark's parents approached me and said, "We want to show you something. Mark was carrying this when he was killed." His father pulled something from his wallet. It was the list of all the good things Mark's classmates had said about him.

"Thank you so much for doing that," Mark's mother said, "As you can see, Mark treasured it."

A group of Mark's classmates overheard the exchange. One smiled sheepishly and said, "I still have my list. It's in my top desk drawer at home." Another said, "I have mine, too. It's in my diary." A third said, "I put mine in my wedding album."

That's when I finally sat down and cried. The lesson my former students taught me that day became a standard in every class I taught for the rest of my teaching career.

Permission given by——Universal Press Syndicate

Teachers have a tremendous impact on the students they touch each and every day in their classroom. Keep this lesson in mind before you begin each day!

Chapter 19

✦

New Year's Resolution: Setting and Attaining Our Goals

o o o o o o o o o o o o o o o o o o o o o o o o o o o o o o

Lost time is never found again.

—Ben Franklin

Every January 1, many people traditionally declare their New Year's resolution(s). Unfortunately, we have seldom attained those goals when the New Year comes to a close. In education, it's imperative that teachers establish a set of goals or objectives in the hope of having a productive school year. Here's a simple approach that can allow you to set goals and then attack them in an orderly fashion throughout the coming year.

Step One: Set measurable, specific resolutions. To make your professional resolutions attainable, they should be quantifiable and measurable and include completion dates or timelines.

For example:
I will collaborate more often with my colleagues in the department to address student-centered learning, assessment, and peer coaching. I'll address these goals on a monthly basis with at least two other teachers.

I will become more proficient in the use of the technology made available in my school district for the purpose of providing my students the best possible learning environment.

I will make an effort to cultivate professional relationships with new teachers during the remainder of the current school year.

I will enroll in graduate classes this year and set aside time on a weekly basis to read current books that address topics in my profession.

Step Two: Break each resolution into achievable sub-goals. Set smaller benchmarks, with specific time tables as to when you will complete that portion of the resolution or goal. This step makes the goal attainable in your mind, and you'll put more effort into seeing it achieved.

For example:
Each week spend thirty minutes after school with one of your colleagues sharing best practices in the area of student-centered learning activities, methods of assessment, technology, classroom management techniques, etc.

Attend a software workshop to ensure you're staying on the cutting edge of how best to incorporate technology into the student learning process or for keeping grades.

Make an effort to communicate weekly with the new teacher(s) during preps, department meetings, lunch, or after school. Offer your assistance, as well as encourage their feedback, to assist one other with school-related projects.

Take one graduate course (three credits) in the fall and one course (three credits) in the spring, working toward a master's degree or other post-graduate degree.

Step Three: Use your calendar or planner to schedule each goal in detail on a monthly basis. This will help you to stay on target. If you can see it daily, you'll have a better chance of meeting that goal. Each month map out specific steps you will complete on your way to achieving those resolutions. Remember, inch by inch, any goal is a cinch.

Step Four: Persevere. The bottom line is: Accomplishing anything worthwhile requires work, monitoring, and follow-through. At the end of every month, assess your progress; make adjustments as needed to ensure success. The end result will be a far greater chance of finally attaining your New Year's resolutions. Good luck, and good planning.

Chapter 20

✦

Building Academic Success Begins with Building Social and Emotional Success

○ ○

You can plant a dream.

—*Anne Campbell*

As educators, our greatest challenge is finding out how to connect our students to the learning and social activities that are taking place daily in our classrooms and career programs. Don't make the mistake of believing that as educators we only need to focus our attention on the academic growth and development of our students. Until our students connect with their teacher and classmates socially and emotionally, very little academic success will occur.

Understanding the link between belonging (social acceptance by our peers and teachers) and academic performance is critical. Students are more likely to avoid high risk or negative behavior when they feel connected to their families and their schools. When a student feels emotional and social connection within the school setting, academic success can and usually blossoms.

When a school has a committed faculty, positive teacher-student relationships, an orderly environment, and a school emphasis on both the academic and social and emotional development of every student, a greater level of student success is produced. As educators, we cannot control what happens in our students' homes or community, but we have significant control over their learning environment.

In the life of an adolescent, the high school years are a period when they need the most support and guidance for social and emotional growth and development. This doesn't mean as educators we need to become their friends. What it means is that we need to be the best possible positive role models for our students. We need to model patience, stick-to-itiveness, empathy, integrity, good attendance, and the ability or skill to listen effectively and reflect before speaking.

Keep in mind that many teens view high school as an interruption in their day. Therefore, attention must be paid to the development of quality social and emotional development programs that enhance a student's ability to integrate their cognitions, emotions, and behavior to meet the demands of schooling as well as of the demands society places on that human being. In other words, schools must offer programs throughout the year that will also focus on providing adolescents the tools needed to deal with social pressures (like alcohol, drugs, sex, etc.). This can be accomplished through assemblies, small group sessions, and one-on-one counseling.

I encourage you to not only pursue the academic growth and development of each student, but to also focus on the social and emotional development of that student. If we succeed in both arenas, we will provide our students with the tools they'll need to live happy and productive adult lives.

Chapter 21

✦

Personalizing the Educational Community

o o o o o o o o o o o o o o o o o o o o o o o o o o o o o
Never underestimate the power of expectation.
—*Bruce Johnson*

Think about a friend or colleague you always turn to for his or her opinion about an important decision you're about to make. Why do you feel close to that person? This is probably a person that listens intently to what you have to say and gives you an honest and sincere response each and every time. So if we want our students to succeed in school, they need to make a healthy and sincere connection between the learner and the learning environment. When this is accomplished, students tend to have greater motivation, increased attachment to learning, and improved achievement, especially those students who are less successful or feel alienated. Positive connections to peers, schools, and learning are all associated with reductions in high-risk behaviors, including acts of violence, drug abuse, and dropping out of high school.

Personalizing learning doesn't mean we become the student's friend. It does mean we'll work very hard to understand how each student learns best and design learning activities that provide the greatest opportunity for success. It promotes relationships formed on a foundation of trust, respect, collaboration, and support. As Theodore Sizer states, "You need to know students well to teach them well, and you need to be passionate about what you teach if students are to value what is taught."

Here are some key factors to help ensure that every student is seen, heard, known, and understood:

- Develop a positive and sincere relationship with your students.
- Model positive peer relationships for your students.
- Create a learning environment where all students feel safe, welcomed, respected, and connected.
- Vary your learning activities so they emphasize choice, voice, collaboration, multiple intelligences, and the social construction of knowledge.
- Use learning tasks that have personal meaning and value.
- Design learning tasks that require higher-level thinking and problem solving.

Improving the quality of relationships among and between educators and students should be the cornerstone of every school. If our kids feel connected, they'll experience a higher level of success. Some educators may not feel comfortable with this idea, but it does work, based on my own experiences in the classroom and those of my colleagues. The kind of personal relationship I'm referring to is one of utmost professionalism. It means we never give up on a student. It means listening (listening with your heart, if need be), reflecting, and then assisting or guiding. Making a connection with our students will promote greater success for both the learner and the educator.

Chapter 22

✦

Pupil Success With Instructional Accommodations

○ ○

Teach your students to reach, and they'll never stay on the ground.

—*Unknown*

We've all heard many times that students have different learning styles. Professional literature reinforces this theory that each child has a unique way of learning. Master teachers must then take the time to understand how their students learn best and accommodate or adjust their instructional techniques. Even federal law (No Child Left Behind) mandates that schools, administrators, and teachers implement instructional strategies that will ensure the success of every student.

Based on several conversations during my career with primary or elementary teachers, it appears high school students receive fewer instructional accommodations as compared to students in grades K through eight. Yet, older students still need effective and appropriate support during their high school years in order to be successful in their studies. Listed below are some strategies teachers can use in an effort to identify the most appropriate accommodations for their students:

- Ask your students *individually* about what helps them learn better and what gets in the way of their showing what they really know and understand. This can be accomplished whenever you have one-on-one contact with a student, in the classroom setting or even outside the classroom.

- Consider the strengths and weaknesses of your students in areas linked to the curriculum or content. Identify those skills or behaviors that seem to consistently get in the way of learning. Then, adjust. One example might be a student who has difficulty keeping up with note-taking during the lecture or demonstration portion of a lesson. Prepare an abbreviated note sheet containing all the key information for the entire class, so all your students can focus on your lecture and demonstration. Some students become easily frustrated trying to listen, watch, and also take careful or accurate notes. The handout will eliminate unnecessary tension and allow students to relax and listen.

- Teach your students how to use their accommodations. If students do not know how to use an accommodation, it will be of no benefit.

- Observe the effects of the accommodations you've provided to determine whether they are being used and the extent to which the accommodation seems to be useful to the student(s). Again, if necessary make adjustments as needed to best support the student's learning.

- Collect both formative and summative data on the effects of the accommodations that are used by or for the individual student. Just as the learning style is different from student to student, realize that one set of accommodations is not going to work well for every student.

- Remember that accommodations not only need to occur in our instructional strategies, but also in the student learning tasks and the forms of student assessment.

- With proper teacher commitment to providing the necessary support for all students, learners can meet the challenges in every classroom.

Chapter 23

✦

Learning from Our Peers

o o o o o o o o o o o o o o o o o o o o o o o o o o o o o o

Man's greatness lies in his power of thought.

—Blaise Pascal

The old adage, "From your pupils you are taught," is true. We can also learn from our peers, and we should. Indeed, we can and should learn from everyone around us. It makes growing as a person and a professional a much easier and richer task.

Educators sometimes look for role models outside the school. That's okay, but don't overlook the successful people in your own professional backyard. There are successful people in our own school who can also contribute to our continual growth.

Look for first-rate models. Identify effective communicators who are active in their community, the most successful in their discipline, and who achieve their goals. Nine times out of ten they will be considered as Master Teachers in your school.

You can also find excellent models outside education (for instance, in business and industry). You'll find they have skills that can be adapted to the classroom setting, especially regarding time management, effective use of technology, charting benchmarks to increase the chances of a positive outcome (with your classroom goals), and interpersonal techniques.

An excellent way to observe professionals from other walks of life is to take a professional day (if your district allows them; if not, take a personal day) and spend the day in quiet observation. Set aside time at the end of that day to discuss what you've observed and ask for clarification, if needed.

Learn how to ask very specific questions. Ask questions about their thinking, beliefs, communication strategies, and action skills. Also, find out all you can about how they manage time, work, and relationships with people in their profession, and then translate what you've heard and seen into an action plan.

Make it a point to identify the specific values held by these people. Discuss the rules they live by and the role their values and character have played in their success. Ask them to define such words as *attitude, integrity,* and *happiness.* You may be shocked or surprised with how much thought they have given to these words.

Successful educators know that they will best learn the secrets of success from people who are successful. But if we associate with professionals who have negative attitudes or lack integrity, we will experience failure and frustration.

The feeling of success is one of the greatest feelings we experience in our profession. We feel successful when we have a sense that we're continually getting better at what we do.

Your school is loaded with successful people. Take advantage of that resource. Learn how to be even more successful from your peers.

Chapter 24

✦

Mid-Point: Time to Assess, Adjust, and Move Forward

○ ○

Be sure you put your feet in the right place, then stand firm.

—*Abraham Lincoln*

The effective management of time is an enormously important skill teachers need to master (with all that needs to be accomplished, we can not afford to waste time). Secondly, we must establish simple and clear classroom rules that all must follow, including the teacher.

At least once each month, we need to take time to reflect on just how effectively we and our students are using time in the classroom. This evaluation should include how we treat one another during discussions, question and answer, and assessment, and adjust our actions when necessary. Is the current atmosphere conducive to student learning or detrimental to the learning process?

Classroom Management Techniques

- Greet your students at the door. Smile and say "Good morning" or "Good afternoon."
- Direct students to their assigned seats. Don't allow them to congregate in small groups in the classroom.
- Reinforce classroom rules (keep them simple) as needed, explain

them, and make sure they are posted (try to limit to between three and six rules).

- Compliment students for their effort, even if their response is incorrect. If you fail to do this, students will be less likely to try again, as they'll feel like a failure.
- Make sure that all of your students are visible all the time. You need to keep them connected to the learning activity. One of the best ways is to make sure your students know you're watching them every minute they're with you.
- The classroom must be neat, clean, and very organized if you wish to establish and maintain a positive learning environment. A messy room tells your students it's okay to lose or damage things or forget to bring them to class.
- Accurately target misbehaving students. Never correct a student in a way that verbally backs them into a corner; never. We're professionals, so correct inappropriate behavior in a professional way.
- Enforce fair consequences for inappropriate behavior. The punishment should always fit the crime. We don't need to use excessive force to stop bad behavior.
- Discipline with empathy.

Instructional Techniques

- Think about the subject matter to be covered, the composition of the student group, and the types of interaction expected.
- Plan lessons that are appropriate and will eventually lead to meeting the final outcome of the course or session.
- Make sure you are addressing the learning styles of all students. Design a multitude of learning activities that will engage every student.
- Make smooth transitions from one activity to another.
- Use signals to prepare students for transitions. Use verbal cues ("At this time, please open your books to page _"), or visual cues (flash the classroom lights on and off a few times).
- Conduct lessons and activities at a reasonable pace, and incorporate student-centered learning activities.
- Avoid long, drawn-out lectures or instructions. Students have a listening span of about ten to fifteen minutes before you start to lose them. Make your lectures brief, but vibrant.
- Vary your questioning techniques.

- Devise creative ways to verify that students are actively participating in the learning activity (question and answer, observation, student questions, a show of hands, inattentiveness, etc).
- Maintain a high level of student involvement.
- Frequently scan the entire classroom to assess the level of student focus on learning.
- Provide constructive feedback.
- Provide extra assistance to students in need.
- Do whatever it takes to make learning interesting and fun.
- Let students take charge of their own learning.
- Nurture a village of learners in your classroom and school.

Chapter 25

◆

How to Handle the Procrastinating Student

○ ○
Some of the best discoveries are made when we simply try.
—*Unknown*

Students that procrastinate can cause us countless hours of unnecessary work and aggravation. Procrastinators always put things off until the very last minute. They feel no sense of urgency. This chapter will examine ways in which we can bring about positive change in those students who seem to always wait until the last minute to complete a task.

One reason for procrastination is the student's need for attention and power. Whenever you communicate with the student procrastinator, you must let him or her know that you do not find this behavior charming or acceptable. Tell the student you don't like the behavior and that it must change. Clearly outline the changes you require. Then, monitor the student on a regular basis to ensure he or she is keeping up with the work.

Other reasons can prevent students from meeting timelines or deadlines set by their teacher. Some students may be dealing with a difficult home life that is directly interfering with them getting school work completed. Meet with the student privately and/or contact the guidance counselor to see what conditions outside the classroom may be affecting a student's effort in class.

Demonstrate to the student how this behavior is giving him or her the opposite reputation of the one he or she may want. Also, explain that always being late and requiring constant prodding hurts him or her as a person, as well as academically as a student.

Establish a timeline for each student to adhere to, and periodically meet with them to check on progress. Constantly reinforce that you will not accept work after the predetermined deadline. You'll also need to contact the parents or parent and get them on board as to their child's ongoing problem. Send a copy (or e-mail it) of the assignment home to the parents so they can follow-up at home. Always encourage the procrastinating student when he or she has met the deadline. The praise will provide the desired attention and stimulate the desire to meet future deadlines.

As you work with student procrastinators, know that getting angry with them is both a waste of your time and ineffective. There are other productive steps you can take to bring an end to their constantly late work. Here are a few suggestions: when asking questions in class, call on them, and try to select a question the procrastinator will be able to answer completely or partially; set benchmarks and check with them on a regular basis; contact the parents to assist you in changing their bad habits; hold students to every deadline; and praise them when they do what is expected of them.

Consider inviting several people who represent business and industry to visit your classroom. Have these speakers address the importance of meeting deadlines and how failure to do so can in many cases mean the loss of a job. Sometimes your students need to hear this message from outsiders for it to really sink in and have an impact.

In closing, the seasoned teacher knows that procrastinating is a habit. Students hold to this behavior because it works for them. It is our job to break them of this habit before they enter the real world. In the end, they will thank you for bringing about an end to this destructive habit.

Chapter 26

✦

Integrity: The Heart and Soul of Every Good Educator

○ ○

If your motive is really to help, you'll find a way to speak the truth.

– Unknown

Each year schools around the country perform a National Honor Society induction program for students who have demonstrated scholarship, leadership, good character, and service to others. These traits make the members of the National Honor Society stand head and shoulders above their fellow classmates.

As educators, the most important trait we need is *integrity*. Educators with integrity come to school ready to work. They have a strong work ethic. Sliding through an hour or a day never enters their mind. They tackle every challenge with every ounce of strength and enthusiasm available to them.

- Educators with integrity care about their students and colleagues. They do more and offer others more than expected. They don't think in terms of what they can get by doing a certain task or assignment. Make no mistake, it is personal integrity that makes them want to help others.

- Educators with integrity have character that can stand up under scrutiny. They are known for their self-imposed and self-regulated positive standards.

- Educators with integrity have the courage of their convictions. They will stand up for what they believe. They will fight for their students. They understand they are here for one reason and that is to promote *powerful instruction*. Their goal each day is to be able to say, "Today my students left class having learned something new."

- With integrity, educators have no reason to be paranoid or fearful. When we hold the best intentions for those we serve (our students) and those we work with (our colleagues), we feel right to pursue our work and involvement in the school community.

- No one will deny that those with high integrity are also highly committed—to student, parents, and the school team.

- Finally, those who have integrity are loyal to people, to missions, and to the school district. They have the ability to make others feel good about themselves. They are sensitive rather than insensitive, inclusive rather than exclusive, and embracing rather than rejecting. Without question, educators with integrity don't wear a badge of honor, they just live it each and every day they come to work.

Chapter 27

✦

Protecting Students from Harassment

○ ○
You can not shake hands with a clenched fist.
—*Indira Ghandi*

Harassment is something that occurs in society. Often it takes place between students in our schools. We need to be aggressive in putting a stop to the harassment children are inflicting on their peers during the bus ride, in the halls and the lunchroom, on the athletic fields, and even in the classroom.

Let's take a moment to define the term *harassment* to reach a clear understanding, especially with regard to schools. Harassment has been defined in recent legal cases as any behavior by students and/or staff that makes for an uncomfortable learning environment. A second legal definition for harassment is the purposeful intent to intimidate, exploit, or hurt another.

Most educators want to do the right thing in an effort to stop hurtful behavior. We need to take a comprehensive approach to ending harassment in our schools. The solution is rather simple; we need to create a school culture that simply doesn't tolerate harassing behavior. If we encourage, by example, a culture that focuses on people treating others with respect, we'll need fewer rules about behavior. However, schools also need to provide ongoing staff development on effective techniques for addressing and deterring harassment. The training also needs to address the legal obligations of school personnel when dealing with harassment cases. As educators, we're not permitted to close an eye or ear to these behavior patterns. They must be addressed at the time they occur.

During the school year, there may be times when a teacher determines an open discussion in class that addresses the topic of harassment is needed. During my career, I witnessed one student bullying another student in my shop program over the use of a piece of equipment. I immediately stepped in and had the "bully" take a seat, waited a few minutes, and then spoke to him (99 percent of the time a male student was doing the bullying) privately in my office. He was warned that if I saw it happening again I would call his parents and send him to the office for a detention or in-house suspension.

These discussions require the teacher and student(s) to follow a set of rules on the way everyone will conduct themselves during the discussion, listen to various viewpoints, identify solutions, and implement new standards that will discourage harassment. Such discussions help create a shared culture that will support an environment of respect because the focus is on communication and consensus building. Whenever possible, the resolution is determined by all parties involved. If students have a stake in the resolution, they're more likely to uphold it. Occasionally, I would involve the student's guidance counselor and or parent(s) if the bullying persisted.

Secondly, educators have the responsibility to model zero tolerance for harassment. The teacher can accomplish this by treating every student, as well as their colleagues, in a respectful manner. Our students are constantly watching our actions and will hold us accountable at a later date. Always treat your students with respect, even the "bully." We know what needs to be done to stop the spread of harassment in schools. If we join together, students and staff, harassment can be eliminated.

Chapter 28

✦

Keep the Passion in Your Teaching

"One person can make a difference and every person should try."

– *John F. Kennedy*

We must not overlook the need for and value of passion in our professional lives. Passion may serve students, parents, colleagues, and us better than any other valued trait. There are many ways to keep the passion burning. Here are just a few ways to achieve that goal: vary the learning activities; encourage interaction with your colleagues; and actively participate in the professional development offered in your district. Passion is the fuel that will run your professional engine most efficiently over the long haul.

By definition, a passion is a deep feeling, a strong emotion by which the mind and heart can be swayed. It is a pursuit to which one must be devoted to in order to lead students toward both learning and the love of learning. We must have passion in our delivery. I found over the years that sitting in on my colleagues' classes gave me new ideas on how to better present new material. Indeed, we simply must have a passion for academic growth and for leading every student, not just some, to achieve.

I decided early on in my teaching career that I would surround myself with the positive-thinking teachers in my school instead of the constant complainers. You know—the ones that see the problems but never offer any solutions. There are a few in every school district. During my career I worked in four different districts, and it didn't take long to identify the naysayers! I made sure to stay clear of those individuals.

The master teacher is very much aware that it's difficult to be an exceptional teacher without the passion to be one. Few of us can be successful at what we do if we do it halfheartedly. We have a professional responsibility in the classroom, but if we don't have the passion, we risk failing. We are the chief executive officer and learning leader in our classrooms, so we need to find and cultivate our passion for learning each and every day of our professional careers. I stress the importance of gravitating toward teachers who are positive in their thinking and actions. Become active in your professional organizations, and keep current with the latest research through periodicals and books in your field. The passion for being an educator lies in the mind and the heart. Fortunately, an educator can inspire the passion for learning and achievement in the hearts of their students and colleagues alike. To keep that passion burning, vary the learning activities, support interaction with your colleagues, and actively participate in professional development. Passion is the fuel that will run your professional engine!

Chapter 29

✦

Self Reflection and Peer Support

o o o o o o o o o o o o o o o o o o o o o o o o o o o o

Allow your opinions to be enriched by the insight of others.

— *Thomas Jefferson*

Teaching is a profession in which dreams are born every day. In our profession, it is vitally important that we keep the dreams we have for ourselves as well as our students alive. What we say each day can light the fire of desire. We've seen it happen throughout our careers in education, and we'll see it happen in the days, weeks, months, and years to come.

Yet we all know how easy it is to stop dreaming. Something happens in our personal life or in the classroom, or a change in school policy sets us back. Then, there are the parents and students whom we just can't seem to connect with, even though we've made numerous attempts.

Take time to step back and reflect on how we have learned to survive. We say to ourselves, "I know I'm a good teacher. I've worked hard to keep my skills current through graduate courses, in-service days, professional workshops, reading educational and career journals, and communication with my colleagues." Another important step we can take to enhance our teaching techniques and expand our methods of student assessment is peer coaching. Peer coaching describes a minimum of two professionals who team up to provide each other with feedback on assessment techniques, instructional methods, classroom management, etc. (If interested in peer coaching, you can find numerous books on the subject).

If your school does not currently utilize a peer coaching approach, contact the administrative team (especially the person or persons responsible for staff development) and discuss implementing peer coaching. Identify other local districts that have peer coaching in place, and send a group from your school to observe and ask questions before initiating a program in your own school or district.

One of the most effective ways we support our own professional skills and confidence is by sharing ideas with our peers. Feedback from our colleagues reinforces our beliefs and enables us to expand our repertoire of teaching styles by exploring untapped resources within ourselves. We learn from one another while planning lessons, developing support materials, observing others working with students, and thinking together. The ultimate goal is teacher autonomy: the ability to self-monitor, self-analyze, and self-evaluate.

Peer coaching provides teachers with a structure that cultivates a deeper level of reflection. This occurs through the conversations we have before and after informal classroom visitations by our colleagues on the peer coaching team. It also becomes a part of our lesson planning and our development of various assessment strategies along with our peer coach. If we become more reflective about teaching, we'll master the skills necessary to handle the daily events that could discourage us from reaching our dreams: encouraging the dreams of our students.

Peer coaching is a powerful process for fostering collegiality, deepening reflective skills, deepening trust, and developing teacher autonomy. The key is pairing teachers with educators they respect who have a proven track record as master teachers, based on both staff input and student feedback.

Chapter 30

✦

Designing Effective Instructional Strategies

○ ○
You know how well you do when you're complimented, so share the wealth with your students.
—*Charles D. Buchheim*

In 2002, the federal government enacted the Elementary and Secondary Education Act, more commonly known as the No Child Left Behind Act. This law requires schools to implement research-based instructional strategies and student-centered learning that will guarantee that every child will succeed.

As educators, we realize that all children have different abilities and interest levels when it comes to learning. So, we work very hard to try to provide every student a sound education.

The ongoing question we must ask ourselves is whether or not our instructional strategies and learning activities have connected with every child in our classroom as we try to guarantee some degree of growth and development each day. Make sure you've collected some hard data or feedback from your students by the end of each class so you can determine as best you can their actual level of understanding. This information will establish your starting point for the next day.

It can be very difficult to truly assess whether or not we're effectively making that connection with every single student we teach. So what can we do to help ensure that Powerful Instruction is taking place, day in and day out?

Here are some steps to assist in designing effective instructional strategies and student learning activities:

- Visit other teachers in your school informally to observe other methods and an assortment of student learning activities first-hand.
- Meet with staff development personnel for brainstorming sessions on the latest instructional methods being used.
- Develop a strong communications network with parents in an effort to keep parents informed about your learning expectations for their child and to discuss how the parents can assist you in identifying their child's learning style(s).
- Take a critical look at your students quality of work (written, oral, group, hands-on, other) being submitted. Ask yourself if the instructional side was adequate or needs to be revised or redesigned or whether your students need to expend additional effort. Assess how you can help bring about that change.
- Display the work students have completed in an effort to motivate them to work even harder.
- Take advantage of in-house and outside professional workshops that will expand your teaching repertoire.
- Enroll in college courses so you can be in touch with the latest theories concerning instructional strategies and effective student-centered learning activities.
- Incorporate both formative and summative assessments in your classroom setting.
- Make a point of sharing what works with your colleagues.
- Examine the new textbooks in your discipline(s) for new ideas and supplemental information that can be incorporated into your instruction and learning activities.
- Be an active participant in professional organization(s).
- Don't become predictable in the classroom. Work hard at making sure your learning activities vary from day to day and week to week

All of us have an obligation to keep ourselves current in our profession. Each of us can do this in different ways. What matters is that we make a daily effort to expand our skills and understanding of how young people learn and take the steps needed to ensure that *no child is left behind.*

Chapter 31

✦

Student Assessment: Hard Data

o o o o o o o o o o o o o o o o o o o o o o o o o o o o o o o o
Don't find fault. Find a remedy.

—Henry Ford

As we come to the end of a lesson, we need to gather information, or hard data, from our students so we can assess just how well our students understand or are able to perform a specific task or skill. One way is to have our students assess themselves by using various methods in the closing moments of the period. When our students become involved in self-assessment, we can begin to clearly observe any learning gaps between what was taught and what students have learned. In addition, when teachers provide time for their students to pause and reflect, they get immediate feedback to help guide future student learning and teacher instruction.

Let's examine a few methods to assess just how much our students really understand as we come to the conclusion of a lesson. We're going to call these assessments *reflective ac*tivities.

- **Pause and Think Notebook** Have your students write responses to one or more phrases listed on the board, such as 1.) What was confusing? 2.) One question I have is … 3.) I'd like to know more about … or 4.) Two things I learned are …
- **Margin Symbols** Create a number of symbols that students can place on a worksheet, homework assignment, test, etc., to express how they feel, such as 1.) This is too hard ! 2.) It's easy. 3.) I know this so well I could teach someone else.
- **Muddiest Point Card** The muddiest point in today's class is …

- **Exit Pass** Two things I learned today are … One question I still have is …
- **Getting There** I think I'm starting to …
- **Before & After Proof** I used to believe … And now I know …
- **Ticket to Leave** On a 3 x 5 card or piece of paper, the student tells the teacher two or three things he or she learned today or responds to a specific question asked by the teacher.

The only way we can determine how our students are doing is to retrieve hard data daily. By reflecting on our students feedback, we can more effectively design or re-design our lessons and student-centered learning activities. When necessary, re-teach the lesson; it's time well spent—especially for the learner!

Chapter 32

✦

Competition Vs Collaboration

○ ○

You are the only one who can stretch your own horizon.

—*Unknown*

Recently, I read an article that examined the question of whether to incorporate competitive activities in your classroom versus collaborative types of activities. In today's accountability-driven world, many of us believe competition is the best way to push our students to work to their full potential. Often, administrators have supported this approach. Well, hold onto your pencils and calculators, because some educators believe that competition is not an effective way to motivate students. In the book *No Contest:* The Case Against Competition, author Alfie Kohn argues that teachers construct competitive activities based on mistaken assumptions. Competition, says Kohn:

- Does not motivate students to do their best;
- Does not build students' character or self-esteem; and
- Does not help students build good social skills.

Competition should not be used to introduce a new idea or concept. Competition seldom leads to meaningful learning. In fact, in competitive classrooms, teachers and students focus on the extrinsic goal of *winning* the competition. However, the real goal of any lesson is to create an intrinsic interest in wanting to learn authentically and understand the idea or concept so it can be applied to future life experiences.

For some students who especially struggle with their learning, competition can feel like constant punishment, perpetuating the notion that school is unfair or unjust. Students will begin to feel that their teacher only wants to teach the brightest kids.

Collaborative learning activities are a better alternative to competition. Creating effective cooperative classrooms takes much effort and prior planning for both the students and teacher, but the outcomes are worth the extra effort. The following five elements provide a foundation for making cooperative learning activities work:

- **Positive interdependence** Students are linked with others so that each one's success depends on the team's combined efforts.
- **Individual accountability** Each student in the group is held accountable through assessments that are shared with the students in the group.
- **Face-to-face interaction** Students help, support, encourage, and praise others in their group as they learn together.
- **Social skills** Students apply skills such as leadership, decision making, trust building, communication, and conflict management within their group.
- **Group processing** Students discuss their common learning goals, the procedures they follow to achieve the goals, and their progress, problems, and success as individuals and as a team.

The key to collaborative learning is to plan ways to involve every student, beginning the first minutes of every class. Pose thoughtful questions that require students to think deeply and share important ideas with fellow classmates, as well as their teacher. Don't be afraid to incorporate higher level thinking skills questions. You'll be surprised how well your students may respond. Cooperative experiences can cement ideas or concepts into your students' memory banks for a lifetime.

Chapter 33

✦

Education: Helping Children Realize Their Potential

Allow your opinions to be enriched by your students.

– Charles D. Buchheim

As teachers, we've all experienced, or will experience, students who interrupt the learning activity with some outburst or rule infraction. As trained professionals, we immediately put into place tactics we hope will curb and eventually stop this distraction. Sometimes they work, and of course, there are times when our strategies fail miserably.

As all teachers do, we know these students quite well. So, we need to dig deeper into the disruptive student's mental and social needs and deficiencies before we can bring an end to this behavior. Without identifying the student's likes and dislikes, strengths and weaknesses, gifts and talents, all efforts will probably fail..

If the student has some real artistic abilities, we might consider giving him the responsibility for making posters that correlate to the issue. If he works better alone than in a group, assign him specific tasks when others move into a group activity. However, eventually he needs to learn how to work in concert with his fellow students; take it slowly, as you have an entire school year. Since he likes attention, call on him for answers even before he raises his hand. Also, call on him when you have an indication that he knows the correct response, in an effort to build his self-confidence and prevent unwanted outbursts.

In time, student outbursts should decrease. Try to remember always that your students are more than a set of behaviors. They are young people who have needs, desires, and preferences. When problems arise, look past the situation and into the child to begin determining appropriate action(s).

Know your students well enough to identify what they need, then give it to them. Choose not to label your students by their behaviors. Help them evolve into something better than they thought they could be.

Chapter 34

◆

Controlling Anger: A Life-long Lesson

○ ○

"Who is wise? He that learns from everyone."

—*Ben Franklin*

Anything we can do to keep students from acquiring negative attitudes and behaviors will give us a distinct teaching advantage. As we all know, negative behavior in the classroom can and will impact learning. Anger halts forward movement. It creates blockages where none should exist.

As educators and role models for our students, we can switch negative attitudes to positive attitudes by using positive words. Try to refrain from using such words as *no, never,* and *but.* Such words can cause instant resistance and defensiveness. Instead, make it a point to use words that imply or convey positive attitudes or actions as well as a sense of responsibility. These positive words are *yes, good,* and *instead of.* Take this approach from day one.

In the same vein, use positive answers and permission-seeking words, such as "May I?" as often as possible to lift students' status. When you want to offer advice or a suggestion, precede your comments with the question, "May I offer you some advice?" By asking students' permission, you enhance their status, create involvement, and give them a measure of authority. Yes, it is simple, but very effective.

Another example of positive phrases you can use to help students retain a positive status when you are urging a student to do something is, "A student of your standing would …."

Another way of affirming students is to say, "As you know ..." before answering a question. This positive phrase implies that students have some knowledge already. Equally important, it makes a positive out of a possible negative.

When students say "It won't work" before they even try, don't argue. Also, don't get angry or try to convince or patronize. If you do, students may lock into the negative. The minute you hear students say, "I can't," reply, "Let's see how many ideas we can come up with before we throw in the towel." Then, hold this positive course and move forward.

Consider turning to your colleagues and begin sharing "Best Practices" within your department or school building. Some colleagues teach the same students you teach, and the same negative conduct probably carries over into the other classes. Talk with those teachers, and find out what techniques they're using to stop the negative habits of that student. Then try using the techniques in your classroom. You'll come away from that experience with new instructional strategies and student-centered learning activities that can improve your students' level of success, as well as adding new strategies to your repertoire of techniques.

Since we're examining how educators can motivate their students to switch from negative to positive attitudes or actions, I ask that you take some time to share with your colleagues how you approach the following situations:

- What positive techniques do you use to mediate student conflicts?
- How do you go about working with negative students?
- How do you change complaints into positive actions?
- What promises do you make to your students?
- How do you create respect between your students and you in the classroom?
- What forms of praise do you use to change negative attitudes into positive ones?

I close with this simple but true thought:

"Teaching is the greatest act of optimism." – *Colleen Wilcox*

Chapter 35

◆

Students Have Their Jobs Too!

o o o o o o o o o o o o o o o o o o o o o o o o o o o o o

When you make a mistake, admit it, learn from it and don't repeat it.

– Bear Bryant

Learning is a two-way street. It takes a combined effort from the instructor as well as the learner or student. Unfortunately, a percentage of school-age children seem to forget that they have a responsibility to put daily effort into their education.

For more years than we wish to acknowledge, educators have had to experience the harsh words of "Joe Public" putting down today's public schools for failing our children. What "Joe Public" fails to see is that policy makers outside the education system (elected officials at the state and federal levels) often make choices that educators are required to implement. Not only must schools comply with these regulations; we often must do so with little money or no funding. All across America the public is turning to educators to solve every societal problem that exists. Parents need to do their job as parents and let schools return to the business of educating.

I often read with interest the many articles and letters outlining what teachers and parents should do to ensure a child's success in school. However, a third factor in this equation is equally vital, and that is the role the student must play to help bring about his or her own success. It is the student's job to make school important.

It is the student's job to take care of his or her social life outside the classroom and pay attention to the lesson or learning activity while inside the classroom. It is the student's job to bring all the school supplies and textbooks he or she will need to participate effectively, day in and day out.

It is the student's job to eat right and get enough sleep (parents too).

It is the student's job to let the teacher know when something is too difficult. Teachers really do want their students to succeed, and often we can help when there is a problem at school or at home when we're made aware of the circumstances or difficulties the student is facing. Part of the student's job is to communicate clearly with their teacher(s) and parents. As teachers, we need to cultivate an environment that will allow a student to come to us (in private) when they need help or professional guidance.

Chapter 36

✦

Keep the Spirit Burning

○ ○
You are too great for small dreams.

—Unknown

Throughout the school year, teachers and administrators have the awesome task of encouraging the spirit to learn and grow academically, emotionally, and physically in our students. We're bursting with energy, ready to incorporate numerous new strategies and fresh ideas so we can keep the momentum going day in and day out.

There will be times when patience and understanding run low. The slump of discouragement begins to settle in, and we look in the mirror and say, "I need to recharge my educational batteries."

A former colleague, Ken Landis, career instructor at Camden County Technical Schools, shared with me a word diagram he developed and posted in his classroom as a subtle way of reminding himself every day of the important role he plays in the lives of his students. I've decided to share Ken's self-motivational tool. It may be just what you need to recharge your batteries.

Teacher

T   *Talk to your students*
E   *Encourage them*
A   *Answer their questions*
C   *Coach them*
H   *Help them succeed*
E   *Energize their minds and spirits*
R   *Respect them and they will respect you*

I hope Ken's philosophy on the teacher's role gives you the will to keep going even when the day seems dark and hopeless.

On days when you wonder why you ever became a teacher, close your eyes and recapture the moment that inspired you long ago to become a *Teacher*. Your students know you care; that's why you are always there for them.

Chapter 37

◆

Walk-Through, or Informal Visitation

◦ ◦
"Grow like a tree, not like a mushroom—invite feedback."
—Unknown

This chapter is focused on the department supervisor or chairperson. Inspired teaching also occurs when those that directly supervise and evaluate teachers effectively provide ongoing professional growth and development. These professionals must make sure their teachers are moving in the right direction based on: 1.) The mandates established under No Child Left Behind, as well as the specific core proficiencies their state Department of Education has identified for each discipline, and 2.) Provide staff the best possible ongoing and scientifically based professional development so they can be effective in the classroom.

In order to provide useful training, the administrative team needs to have a clear picture of each teacher's strengths and weaknesses. One way of identifying these traits or skills is through frequent visits into the classroom, referred to as *Walk-throughs* or *Informal Visitations*. This can be a very effective way of helping teachers become master teachers. This form of professional development, should focus on small changes, not major readjustments, are sought. Observe how a teacher begins class, prepares materials for a lab or hands-on activity, oversees question and answer exercises, addresses a class disruption, etc.

Here are some reasons why the walk-through can be beneficial to the teacher:

- Frequent observation of a teacher's skills gives greater validity to the feedback over time.
- Frequent visitations lower teacher apprehension over time, making informal visitations as well as formal observations more effective for both parties.
- The more a supervisor knows about how teachers are functioning and making decisions, the more they understand how to approach teachers and offer assistance.
- The more one observes, the more one learns, and the greater the repertoire of strategies one can share with staff.
- Over time, the informal visitations demonstrate firsthand how effective the staff development endeavors have been and where adjustments need to be made.

It is essential that collegiality between instructor and the administrative team develops to improve the various instructional practices. Conducting walk-throughs, or informal visitations, is a valuable vehicle to support or promote collaborative, reflective dialogue within the school environment.

Chapter 38

✦

Student Self-assessment

° °
No one can make you feel inferior without your consent.
—*Eleanor Roosevelt*

One very effective form of assessment is known as *self-assessment*. What does self-assessment look like? There are many ways students can assess their own work. For example, students are involved in self-assessment when they:

- Talk with their teacher about a science lab, or first draft of an essay, or the materials needed to build a birdhouse.
- Have a discussion with a classroom partner on how they arrived at an answer in mathematics.
- Write a response into their log at the end of class or complete a "Ticket-To-Leave."
- Summarize orally or in writing the reasoning used to defend a social position being examined in social studies class.

Self-assessment activities can be accomplished in a relatively short period of time of between one and three minutes; as the complexity increases, assessment may take much more time. This effective type of formative assessment enables teachers to determine each student's level of understanding.

How does self-assessment support student learning? When students assess themselves, they begin to develop insights into their own learning. Rather than relying on feedback from the teacher, through practice they must learn to become reflective at a higher degree. They begin asking themselves,

"Is this right?" "Is this long enough?" "Am I doing it right?" When students are involved in self-assessment, they provide themselves with regular and immediate descriptive feedback that guides their learning.

"How does self-assessment support teachers?" When students are involved in self-assessment, their teachers can identify the gaps between what they have taught and what students truly understand. Observing and interacting with students actively engaged in self-assessment will enrich the depth and variety of the data about student learning.

Additionally, when teachers provide time for students to assess their own learning on a regular basis, students have time to reprocess the information and connect the new learning with past learning experiences. Providing students time to pause and think, proof their work, and connect to the final objective allows teachers to slow the pace of their teaching to match the speed of student learning.

Teachers don't have to, and shouldn't, be the only one evaluating or assessing student progress. Self-assessment is an effective technique to make students more responsible for their learning.

Self-Assessment and Goal Setting by Kathleen Gregory, Caren Cameron, and Anne Davies provided the material used in this chapter. If you would like to examine in more depth self-assessment, consult a copy of this book.

Chapter 39

♦

Ixnay on the Lecture, Lecture, Lecture Approach

The love of learning is cultivated through encouragement, not fear.

—*Vicki Caruana*

Today's students can, at times, be a tough audience for a teacher. It's easy to feel we must be entertainers to hold their attention. Student attention spans seem to be shrinking. Given this reality, how are we to conduct our classes so they are truly effective in motivating our students to learn, to reflect, or problem solve, individually as well as in teams?

The solution is quite simple. First and foremost, we need to know exactly what we want our students to learn. Secondly, we need to break our class or lesson into three distinct parts: the beginning, the middle, and the end.

The beginning should take no more than ten minutes at the opening of your class. This is a critical segment of time, the one and only chance you have to hook the learners. This is when you have to do your best acting, pulling out all the tricks in your hat to ignite their desire to learn, to interact. Attempt to limit your lecture by incorporating discussion and show-and-tell; add technology and visual aids, etc. What ever you do, don't stand in the front of the classroom and lecture, lecture, lecture.

The middle is the largest segment of time. This is when student-centered learning activities take over. Your students will learn and retain much more by doing, not by sitting in their seats taking notes. Organize students into small groups (three is perfect, but four is workable), step back and observe their interactions, listen to their comments and questions, and assess how each group and each student solves problems.

The final segment is the end. This is when you use various soft assessment methods to pull from your students exactly what they have learned or determine their level of understanding. The collection of this data will provide you with the information you need to determine where to begin the following class. Don't stand in front of the class before the bell and recite what you think they understand. It's imperative that you allow your students to state exactly what they understand.

Brendan Francis was once quoted: "Boredom is the bitter fruit of too much routine or none at all." If we are to hold the attention of today's student, we need to effectively plan and implement a variety of learning strategies. We also need to let go of the idea that "I am the teacher, the almighty one, so listen to me and take notes, notes, and notes."

Chapter 40

◆

The Substitute Teacher Can Be Our Friend, with Proper Planning

There're few things as uncommon as common sense.
—*Frank McKinney Hubbard*

Whenever we're absent from school, whether due to illness, a personal day, or attending a professional workshop, teachers worry about how our students will conduct themselves for the substitute teacher. We ask ourselves the following questions; 1.) Did I leave adequate plans? 2.) Will the substitute teacher effectively implement the lesson, and can he or she connect with my students? 3.) What condition will my classroom or shop be in when I return? and 4.) Will the administration have to speak to me about students that were sent to the office? Let's face it, as teachers, all of us have felt these feelings and others when we're away from our students.

During our absence from the classroom, how can teachers and administrators greatly reduce all these concerns and at the same time provide the best possible learning environment for not only our students but for the substitute teacher as well? This chapter addresses some simple, but concrete steps educators should consider implementing to have productive learning taking place when a substitute takes over.

Steps the Team Needs to Take

- Make sure your district involves both teachers and the administrative team in interviewing and hiring the substitute teaching staff.
- The district should provide an in-service program for newly hired substitute teachers to review important board policies and administrative guidelines.
- Develop and provide each substitute teacher with a district *Substitute Handbook*. This handbook should address things like: fire drill procedures, lockdown procedures, how to reach the school nurse, how to reach the assistant principal's office, the policy on passes, using the bathrooms, going to the library, and the technology policy, to name a few.
- Implement an evaluation form that the substitute teacher can complete and submit to the principal's office that addresses: quality of the teacher's substitute plans, seating chart, and condition of the classroom or shop.
- Finally, the administration should conduct ten to fifteen minute walk-throughs of the substitute teacher's classes to observe first hand his or her effectiveness (especially in classes that contain difficult students).
- As in many cases, the classroom's attitude and behavior reflect what teachers expect of their students during their absence. Students need to understand that they are always expected to complete the assignment, as well as maintain good conduct while under the supervision of a substitute teacher.

Steps Teachers Need to Take

- Provide the substitute teacher with a current seating chart that includes the picture and name of each student; today's technology makes this an easy task to complete. List a few positive traits and skills each student possesses. A few examples are: artistic, honest, leader, quiet but capable, strong reading skills, prefers hands-on activities, etc. This could help the substitute make a positive connection with your students. Revise as necessary as your class list changes because of student drops and additions. Make sure you indicate if you have any students that need special accommodations so the substitute can be more effective and helpful.
- **Don't** leave a long reading assignment, followed by writing. This will turn off your students and contribute to behavior problems. Take

what your discipline or subject is currently addressing and design learning activities that are student-centered. Organize students down into groups of three to five to read a short topic and then have a debate. The substitute is the facilitator. Make sure you've provided in your lesson plans the rules students will follow during this activity (the rules should be the same ones you utilize when you're in the classroom). At the end of the debate activity, have each group write a three- to five-sentence paragraph that clearly expresses their final position on the topic. Finally, the students will be informed that their written response will be graded and that everyone in the group will receive the same grade. Also, have the substitute write a comment on each group's written response about their level of positive participation, and score between one (poor) and four (excellent). Team up with other teachers to brainstorm and develop other unique student-centered learning activities for your substitute lesson plans. In the long run, this extra effort will pay back big dividends!

- If possible, call your school the morning you will be out and ask to speak directly to your substitute teacher. This will give you an opportunity to review the assignment and answer any last-minute questions the substitute may have and improve the chances of an effective lesson during your absence. You may want to call your substitute the night before to review the lesson. Ask your principal for the substitute's home phone number or e-mail address. The more you communicate with the substitute, the greater the chances of a successful coverage during your absence.

- Ask your administration to permit you to request a specific substitute teacher both you and your students seem to work well with, in an effort to provide a positive learning experience.

- Finally, the returning teacher also needs to evaluate the effectiveness of the substitute teacher. Design and implement a form (with input from the teaching staff) that is completed by the teacher upon his or her return to school and forwarded to the principal. Provide substitutes with a copy of the form so they know what is expected of them during your absence from class. Some items that should be considered for the form include:

    1. Complete attendance sheet daily.
    2. Place assignment on the board, as well as handing out a copy of the assignment (available in teacher's mailbox or on teacher's desk).
    3. Collect assignment about three minutes before the bell, and ask if there are any questions.

4. Have students place all trash in the classroom container and place chairs under their desks.
5. Provide a list of student(s) sent to the office and the reason why they were removed from the classroom. Complete required misconduct form and submit to assistant principal's office.
6. Place all materials into teacher's mailbox in main office (follow specific instructions left by teacher).

There are two critical teacher contributions that increase the effectiveness of a substitute teacher: 1.) Leaving the classroom or shop in an orderly fashion the day before with all necessary materials available for the substitute, and 2.) Providing effective substitute lesson plans. An effective lesson plan is one that the substitute teacher understands and can facilitate because he or she was given the necessary tools or supplies, classroom setting, and a learning activity that excites your students. It's imperative that educators develop an effective level of communication with substitute staff and an appreciation for the tasks they are expected to implement.

About the Author

A seasoned educator with experience in curriculum development, grant writing and implementation, and administrative leadership, but first and foremost a classroom instructor and peer coach. He loved working with students in three secondary school districts as both teacher and coach for thirty-four years. He earned his bachelor's degree in industrial education and a minor in graphic design at the University of Central Missouri. His graduate studies were completed at Rowan University, where he earned a master's degree in Administrative Leadership. He completed additional course work at Temple University.

During his career, Chaz was a classroom instructor, department supervisor, director of instruction, assistant principal, and principal. He also served as president of the Camden County Principals and Supervisors Association; commissioner of the Olympic Conference; New Jersey State chairman for the Principal of the Year Committee; and president of the New Jersey Association of Industrial Educators. He presented a paper at a national education forum in Washington, D.C., in 2000 on student retention, is a published author in the New Jersey Principals and Supervisors Association (NJPSA) publication, and a contributing photographer for *The History of Runnemede, New Jersey, published by the Borough of Runnemede, 1981.*

Since retiring in the summer of 2006, Chaz has focused his attention on the completion of his first book, *Inspired Teaching.* The forty chapters are a collection of monthly inspirational articles Chaz wrote during the last ten years of his career. He focused each monthly article on connecting with students, motivational instructional techniques, and the importance of varied and effective assessment of students. Additionally, he completed certification to be a mentor for new principals via NJPSA's Leader2Leader program.

Chaz has been married to his wife, Judy, (a second grade teacher and registered nurse) since August 1971. Their son, Jeff, is a Ranger instructor at Fort Benning, and their daughter, Jessica, is a seventh grade English teacher. Teaching truly runs in this family!

The key factor that separates successful teachers from those who doubt their effectiveness comes down to connecting with students, a connection cultivated through inspired teaching. When you're educated, dreams are attainable. So, as educators we need to get our students excited about what they are about to learn.

Chaz B.

Thank you.

Charles D. Buchheim
Inspired Teaching

Books That Inspired & Motivated Me

- A Better Beginning . . . Supporting and Mentoring New Teachers by Marge Scherer
- Blink . . . The Power of Thinking Without Thinking by Malcolm Gladwell
- Building Academic Success on Social and Emotional Learning by Joseph E. Zins, Roger P. Weissberg, Margaret C. Wang, and Herbert J. Walberg
- Cooperative Learning by Dr. Spencer Kagan
- Good to Great by Jim Collins
- High Schools on a Human Scale . . . How Small Schools Can Transform American Education by Thomas Toch
- Instruction for All Students by Paula Rutherford
- Mastery Teaching by Madeline Hunter
- Outliers . . . The Story of Success by Malcolm Gladwell
- The Answer to How is Yes . . . Acting on What Matters by Peter Block
- The Human Side of School Change . . . Reform, Resistance, and the Real-Life Problems of Innovation by Robert Evans
- The Three-Minute Classroom Walk-Through by Carolyn J. Downey, Betty E. Steffy, Fenwick W. English, Larry E. Frase and William K. Poston, Jr.
- The Tipping Point . . . How Little Things Can Make a Big Difference by Malcolm Gladwell
- The Right to Learn . . . A Blueprint for Creating Schools That Work by Linda Darling-Hammond
- The Students Are Watching . . . Schools and the Moral Contract by Theodore R. Sizer and Nancy Faust Sizer

This is just a sampling of the many great books that have influenced my teaching, mentoring and leadership during my career in public education.

Memobooksit

CPSIA information can be obtained
at www.ICGtesting.com
Printed in the USA
FFOW03n1044270418
46387388-48117FF